Whose Flesh is Flame, Whose Bone is Time

Whose Flesh is Flame, Whose Bone is Time

V. Penelope Pelizzon

WAYWISER

First published in 2014 by

THE WAYWISER PRESS

Bench House, 82 London Road, Chipping Norton, Oxon OX7 5FN, UK
P.O. Box 6205, Baltimore, MD 21206, USA
http://waywiser-press.com

Editor-in-Chief
Philip Hoy

Senior American Editor
Joseph Harrison

Associate Editors
Dora Malech Eric McHenry Clive Watkins Greg Williamson

A CIP catalogue record for this book is available from the British Library

ISBN 978-1-904130-60-4

Printed and bound by
T.J. International Ltd., Padstow, Cornwall, PL28 8RW

Acknowledgments

My thanks to the editors of publications where these poems first appeared, sometimes under other titles or in earlier forms:

At Length: "Early," "Late," "Soft Power," "The Monongahela Book of Hours"
Del Sol Review: "Human Field"
The Hudson Review: "To Certain Students," "Suspect"
The Kenyon Review: "Where the Arrows Fell"
The Missouri Review: "The Ladder"
The New England Review: sections from "The Monongahela Book of Hours"
Poetry: "Seven Psalms," "Blood Memory," "Nulla Dies Sine Linea," "Postscript"
Poetry Daily: "Nulla Dies Sine Linea," reprinted April 2012
The Southeast Review: "Songs for the Boisterous Month"
Zócalo Public Square: "Famously Beautiful City"

Human Field, a selection of ten poems from the manuscript, was awarded the 2012 Center for Book Arts chapbook prize and printed in a letterpress edition.

"Seven Psalms," "Human Field," and "To Certain Students" appear in *From the Fishhouse: An Anthology of Poems that Sing, Rhyme, Resound, Syncopate, Alliterate, and Just Plain Sound Great* (Persea, 2009).

"Seven Psalms" is included in *The Best American Spiritual Writing* (Mariner Books, 2006).

"Songs for the Boisterous Month," "Where the Arrows Fell," and "Human Field" are included in the anthology *Poetry 30: Thirty-Something Thirty-Something American Poets* (Mammoth Books, 2005).

The Hiroshige triptych from "The Monongahela Book of Hours"

appears in *Image/Word*, an anthology celebrating works from the Maier Museum of Art at Randolph-Macon Women's College, 2005.

Sections from "The Monongahela Book of Hours" were awarded the 2003 Campbell Corner Poetry Prize and appear in "The Language Exchange: Writing on History, Language, and Contemporary Culture," a web forum at Sarah Lawrence College.

Writing time and privacy was supported by organizations to which I am deeply grateful: The Amy Lowell Travelling Scholarship, The Solo Writers Fellowship/Greater Hartford Arts Council, The Lannan Foundation, The Connecticut Commission on Culture and Tourism, University of Connecticut's Humanities Institute and English Department, The Vermont Studio Center, The Pennsylvania Council for the Arts, The Sewanee Writers' Conference.

Thank you for the sparks Andy Abell, Sabino Berardino, Russ Comeau, Nicole Cuddeback, Camille Dungy, Beth Frost, Charles Mahoney, Shara McCallum, Tracy Roberts-Pounds and Tim Pounds, Jane Satterfield, Wael Sawah, Dana Shiller and Tom Marshall, Nancy West, Roger Wilkenfeld. Thank you, Bob Hasenfratz, for Suetonius and fire. My gratitude to Sharon Dolin, Phillis Levin, Jacqueline Osherow, and Elizabeth Spires for encouragement. For your enthusiasm, thank you Phil Hoy and the editors at Waywiser Press. I'm blessed to have as ideal readers Averill Curdy, Tony Deaton, Karen Holmberg, and Mark Rowe.

For Tony, compass

Lion-like, in roars the month but turns to lamb
And, soft-nosed, snuffs the changing wind:
The dying emperor plucking figs from the stem;
A boy in Nazareth cutting his finger badly on an axe.

And from far Tomis one exile writing *Joy to me is snow*
Made soft by spring/And water on the pond instead of ice,
Hoping ships will dock and bring last winter's
Letters from his wife. Heating himself a bowl of
Fermented mare's milk. Reminding himself (twice)
Barbarus hic ego sum. *Here, I am the barbarian.*

Contents

I

II

III

IV

V

I

Seven Psalms

1

Pain's first casualty is proportion.

So my brother, juror in a child pornography trial,
Browses my shelves while the Easter lamb roasts

And, coming on Weston's nudes of his son
Paired with a text describing how Neil at eight

Is "moulded with reedlike flow of unbroken line"–
The exposures framed so the torso, pentelic marble,

Ends with arm buds and the stem of the penis –
Slams the book and storms out,

Shaken that I own such things.

2

The damaged man licking sauce from his spoon –
Why do I feel stricken sitting in the same café
Watching his unbridled relish in the mess?
He's showing me a secret I don't want to see:
The toughest shell conceals the tenderest meat.

My friend rejects aids to help him hear
Because they transmit chat he's never
Learned to filter out. How do we bear
Any sense without muting its tone?
The cuff of meat around the marrow bone.

3

The clergy who rejected Caravaggio's "Death of the Virgin"
For showing the bare soles of Mary's feet
Could hardly conceive the Holy Mother
Straining like a ewe in labor with the Lamb of God.

Yet Luke writes that the inn was full and the birth outdoors.
A beast's entry. No bed for Heaven's Queen but a nest of straw;
The babe's head haloed but, if we take the incarnation at its word,
Breaching the labial tissue crowned in beads of blood.

The first mystery is spirit housed in meat. And the miracle:
You love the brutal creature eating from your breast.

4

"Nice day," she remarks of the glacier-sharp noon beyond the
    window.
"A nice day, under glass." Backhoeing a new well, her son's

Unearthed a Venetian Whiteheart, the beads-for-beaver currency
Once swapped here by the river, six glass nubs per finished pelt.

Resembling a drop of arterial blood, it's crossed three centuries
And countless palms to this snub of cotton in the vitrine by their
    TV.

He lets me hold it, and the red seed plunges me into a vitreous
Humour where we're all flecks floating in the eye of God.

Then drafts whistle through their window's glazing. Like glass,
My faith's both brittle and liquid, ever shattered or shifting shape.

5

Weeping for help, the devil is plaintive.
He calls us by name and it's unclear what we should do.
I say "should," because if there really is a devil
Gulping in fevered sobs under the bed,
Mustn't there be a God who shut him in our house?

Are we to show pity for the pitiless,
Prove his nature to bite won't stifle our nature
To comfort his wounds? Or is giving the whimpering
Little fiend a blanket and cup of milk a sin?
Which hell do we want to burn in if we're wrong?

6

There was a horse farm, long white paddocks, beside the railroad.
Can you see where this is going? Those horses were beautiful and
    – fresh clover,
Loose fence posts – hard to keep safe. The day two mares and a
    gelding
Stopped an express (no humans hurt, train delayed while the track
    was cleared),
My brother slipped off to the scene. He craved blood, I think,
    because he'd
Reached the age that needs to feel beyond doubt that the world is
    real.

A boy, ten or twelve, on a bike; some horses; a train.

From the blue it comes back, and when I recall his crazy bravado,
    describing

What remained of the giants that once lipped apples from our
    palms, I'm surprised
By my rage: Who'd put horses there? Who a railroad? Who a boy?

7

Such frenzy! All this fluster, no stillness at the root.
Always weeping, raging, driving backhoes, giving birth...

You love illuminated books because they're crammed, like your
Little verse, with busyness. You want the world's
Scraps on velvet, so you've built a reliquary out of words.

Ach, peddler, you're no better than the friar
Hawking pig-knuckles as the bones of a saint.

You want a form that will hold the river's water
So it glitters, miraculous as tears?

First, smash the vial. First, swallow the shards.

Self Portrait as Bronze

Across the bay's mirror a wherry arrows.
Traveler with pointed eyes, follow.
Or, on this bed of sand, sleep
Beside a bronze girl drowned for centuries.

The sea has wept my faïence pupils away,
Which passed long hours watching shadows
Fingering the Flemish tapestries
Covetously while cardinals debated the color of smoke.

Once, startled by the reek of a nuncio's monkey
Capering on its pearled leash,
A mouse slipped from the wainscot
To shelter in my hollow body.

She nested in my elbow's crook.
Bitter winter drafted the hall, but her
Small presence warmed the metal.
It was like having a soul.

Princes admired me and we were sent abroad,
Crated like a wooden egg in the wooden
Bowels of a carrack with snapping white wings.
Then we were salt crumbs

Gnashed in the storm's teeth, until the hold
Cracked and waves tossed the cargo down
Triumphantly as a winning hand
On the baize of the weedy bottom.

Tides carried the fickler treasures away.
But not her. She is so loyal.
Her bones are white coral
Inside the arm where you rest your head.

Self Portrait as Bronze

Now from the same depths, traveler, you and I
Gaze up at the constellations of bubbles
Boats scatter across our green sky.
I try to fathom from their patterns a future,

To imagine us circling beneath them
Like a nomad world, as I heard the astronomer
Summoned before the Pope insist ours is,
Roving a desert path between the stars.

It dizzies me. Do you believe we might be so
Alone? Better those lights were diamonds
Blood-flecked on a pontiff's breast
And winking as he howls, or glints

Off dervish blades reeling for the kill, or torches
Clutched in panicked hands fleeing
The assassination. Anything but fires
Untended and indifferent.

When winds beat the sea I feel her,
Persistent relic,
Scraping within me. Watchful. Troubled.
Tell me, what is that, if not a soul?

Blood Memory

Hunched in the bath, four ibuprofen gulped
        Too late to dull the muscle cramping
          To sate a god who thirsts
      Monthly for his slake of iron,
I am just a body bleeding in bad light.

But after an hour, as the wrenching wanes,
I run more water in, remembering
        When I was a girl my mother knew
            One cure for this pain
            And, while I cried,
        Carried me mugs of tea and whiskey
          Clouded with sugar cubes.

In a palm of pinkish water, I scoop up
        A burl of my flesh, almond-sized.
          The tissues settle, livid
Red to nearly black as I tilt my hand
          Against the light to see it
Glistening like a ruby cabochon,
           Appealing as it appalls,
         Recalling one future, years ago,
        That would have borne itself on my blood
           Had I allowed.
        The question swims into view:
Would I harbor another life now?

Last spring, I sat above the harbor in Naples
          With three friends whose children,
        After a week's vacation, were all
Safely back at school. Palpable,
           The holiday mood
        A morning freed from offspring brought!
(I'd felt a guilty pleasure I'd go home
          Not to cook someone's lunch,

But to read.)
Still, it wasn't long before our talk's
Compass needle trembled North
Toward the Motherland:
Soccer games in the Flegrean fields,
Ancient sun
Reborn and swaddled putto-pink
In mist above the fumaroles;
Rococo
Messes of gelato;
First words, whose honeyed gravity
Weighed on me
Like a toddler's head
Snugged below my chin in sleep.

Then, Serena described
Troubles at her daughter's school.
Their new principal refused to pay
The local gang's protection money.
And so, the teachers
Arrived at work one day to find
The hutches where the children kept
Rabbits and a little clutch of chicks
Overturned.
From the playground swings
The throat-cut animals hung.
Next time we come for you
Someone had written across the door in blood.
Now parents wanted
The principal to pay;
That was how these things were done.
Screw her ideals,
Serena heard.
That bitch is going to get our children killed.

A blade bossed with oyster floats,
The harbor glinted below Serena's voice.
Into that water, Apicius wrote,
        The Romans tossed slaves
To glut the eels they'd later eat
With *tits and vulvae, succulently cooked,*
        Of sows who'd aborted their litters.

                And from that water,
                Fishermen pulled a girl
                        Who'd been under
                        At least a week.
        She may have been the missing one
        The papers were reporting on,
                Whose photo showed her
        Lippy, grinning, seventeen.
                A week in that wake.
        She was scoured of identity.

                Water's thick in Naples
                        As martyr's blood
                Rusting in ampoules in the cathedral,
Where it liquefies on schedule
                        – And it *does*;
                        I've seen the miracle –
                        To show the city's
                Still protected by the saint.

        I can't remember, six months later,
        Loggy in my cooling bath,
If some net had hauled these images
                Writhing up at me that morning
                        As we sat together
                                Near the harbor,
                Or if they'd tangled in my thoughts

That same evening after Serena's dinner
              Honoring Women's Day.
                    Across Europe
Lapels flickered yellow wicks of mimosa,
                Marking the feast.
               And in Naples
           Flowers fumed for women
Burned on the flank of Mt. Vesuvius,
                  Where they'd been sewing
Sweatshop zippers on fake designer bags.

        But as it did with everything,
The city managed to transubstantiate
          Horror into carnival.
            With Theresa and Ellie
      I'd walked home late along the harbor.
Fireworks seethed above the bobbing masts.
        Mirroring those harrier stars
        The water seemed to flame, while
              Drowned in lights
The lungomare phosphoresced.
          Scooters rippled through
             Reefs of cars,
      Barely slowing for schools of boys
              And women in flocks,
         Stiletto-heeled, who stalked
Screeching over the cobblestones.
              From an alley's mouth
          A gobbet of men disgorged.
One, drunker than the others, loomed
        Over and bent his face to mine.
            Where are your babies? he hissed,
            Spit pricking my skin.
               Get home to your babies.
      Not just drunk but whetted, his glare

Stropped beyond seeing and testing its edge.
You're over the hill
For trolling – is that what he meant?
Or was he putting all women away,
Including the vampire-
Lipsticked teens?
Whatever he meant, he meant to make us bleed.

I wince, drain chill water out,
Drizzle in a little
More of the hot,
And wonder at this habit
Of holding others' words as worry stones
To fidget absentmindedly
When thought goes slack.
Agates of fury, quartzes of scorn.
Cold in my ear's palm
The hematite heaviness of a final *no*.

And I still turn over my mother's words,
Costly pearls
Handed me years ago
In a college project on oral history.
She took my assignment seriously,
Agreeing to an interview
As if it would allow
Her, too, to wash
Through the wrack of half-forgotten truths.
Painstakingly on tape
She recorded her life,
Lapped by sluices and hesitations.
Her years in the Women's Army Corps,
Screening films on safety and hygiene
To bored enlisted men.

Her depression.
Decades as a secretary. Marriage.

Until, near side B's close, there gathered
A final, muscled wave:
How, when she was well past forty,
Her bleeding stopped.
At first she thought it was her age.
Then, slowly, sickly,
She understood.

She'd tried to find
A doctor who would help her, but
(Her voice cresting, breaking)
Five months along, it was too late,
Even if she'd had the money.
The tape's hiss like receding surf.

So here I am, at daybreak,
Adjusting the taps with my toes.

I think we are shelled animals,
Hauled at by tides, sleeking invasive grit
With our nacre. I think of her
Hiding in the tub for half an hour
To read; think how pleased
I was, finding her, to pull her
Back to me.

Little plumes of my flesh rock in the swells
But my body is bland now,
Yielding as kelp,
And with my toes I pull the plug.

Drained, I need a couple hours of sleep,
> Then I'll start the day again.
> And maybe, if I'm sleeping late,
>> The dream will come,
>> One that intrigues me almost
> More than it disturbs, in which
>> I'm falling, bound,

Into a bay of blood-threshed water.
>> Fear ties me; brine
> Bites my lungs and I can't breathe.
> Then, with a clarity I mistake
>> For waking, I wake
> Below trees, at a table laid
>> Variously with meats –
>> Meats I realize,
> From a shudder in the grove's air,
>> Are human.
> It should be awful; it *is* awful.
>> But with a calm

Familiar only here, a calm
I've never known in any other place,
> I find myself longing to taste
>> The dish's savor,
> Braised and stuffed, as Apicius writes,
>> With larks' tongues.

Nulla Dies Sine Linea

On my birthday

A crow guffaws, dirty man throwing the punch of his
One joke. And now, nearer, a murder

Answers, chortling from the pale hill's brow.
From under my lashes' wings they stretch

Clawed feet. There the unflappable years
Perch and stare. When I squint, when I

Grin, my new old face nearly hops
Off my old new face. Considering what's flown,

What might yet fly, I lean my chin
On the palm where my half-cashed fortune lies.

II

The Ladder

In the wolf's mouth.

In the lion's den.

In the storm's eye.

Under Time's wing.

Let me choke the wolf.

Let me skin the lion.

Let me blind the storm.

And from Time's wing

Let me pluck the feather

That sends it flying.

≈

The Ladder

Again, sweet season, come again, come with red
Crowning over the hill, tip the maple wands with red,
Mark their sugars rising. Nature's first green is red,

Red the thorn-brake where the buck has hung his head,
Red stain blushing under saplings' bark,
Red the restless cardinal's crop.

From light's slow slight lengthening out

Come nipple-jut and pulse along the throat,
Taut belly's proof and urge of hottest blood
Quickening among the changing winds.

≈

Little hooks soled the bee's shoes,
My father said, so she could scale the ladder
My fingers made as nimbly as I climbed stairs.
We watched her ambling along my thumb.

By the waking hive we drowsed. Like pollen
Blown across a field, bees lifted from its mouth,
Tuning their wing's vibrations to the season.
Sun-honeyed near that ardent mind, I heard

Murmurs of a story I half-remembered
In tongues half-familiar through wholly foreign.

≈

Zero year in Rome. The cattle trade runs cheap. A fertile spring
Hooves every market town with calves. For slaves, too, prices are
   low.
Publius Ovidius Naso, leaving the circus after seeing men turned

To beasts, thinks *Now I am ready to sing of bodies changing form.*
Celts sharpen iron blades along the empire's edge, and nightly
Through the east a comet drags its rouged, portentous chariot of
   sparks.

O Ancients, a few centuries till your gods lived in their star-struck
Names alone. Could you read that future in the entrails of a cock?

And we who've freed the atom's genii from its lamp – are we more
   literate,
Scrying through the microscope the scripts curled in our cells?

≈

The Lone Star State. Here it's oil, not coal,
They pull from underneath the hills. Still,
What's a middle-aging cowgirl when you subtract
Boots, spurs, two-step, and her highest hopes?
Carbon plus its stumbles. So the geneticist scanning
This pregnant wrangler's fetal cells for mis-steps
Feels a spin of pleasure when, cheek-to
Cheek, all the chromosomes pair up
Without a wallflower on the slide. Two Xs.
Oh girl, oh sweet the geneticist croons with her radio.

≈

Shit-shod, glar-nosed, once more he hid
  Between flanks in the byre when music went round.

But this time the creature would not spare him.
  *S*ING ME SOMETHING, C*AEDMON*.   Calmly

With a silver finger it preened oil of violet
  Through its fiery wings.   C*AEDMON?*

But, stammered the shepherd, *I know no song!*   C*AEDMON, SING*
  THE LADDER.   *A ladder?*   *T*HE LADDER.

Into his throat he felt warm oil seeping until
  Locks turned
                Measured the Maker

A ladder whose legs   *lengthened and spiraled.*
  Rung after rung,   *ringing like strings*

Fretted by fingers,   *it fleshed into form*
  The Maker's music   *with modulations.*

Though toothed Time   *tears the hours,*
  Devours days and   *down the ladder*

Razes each rung,   *rejoice regardless.*
  Safe in each small cell   *swells the first song.*

Alone again, speechless on dawn's frosted hem.
  Cows cudding. Savor of violets.

≈

High amid twigs now trembling green, the library opens
One glass eye. Spring summons me from my page to attend
Her fluent digressions. Veering to madness on such a day,
Virginia Woolf would catch the swallows at her window
Arguing in Greek, though when Saint Francis called them
Little sisters, they spoke his local tongue.

How plausible all language seems for these
Handfuls of hollow bone and feather, steering
Via blood memory and synaptic star-chart
Three thousand miles north to voice us free of winter.

≈

I am a sturdy pinion of goose, quoth the first pen
Snug in the monk's satchel. *My plume is rich;*
Devotedly the scribe takes me in hand and my nib
Fills the vellum page with joyous meaning.

Likewise I, spoke the swan's quill, *gave up*
My flight to serve Our Lord. Behold the majuscules
Embellished here! The moon shone white
On my wing whose feather now shapes His Word.

The third pen, cut from a crow, was silent.
It knew the Word was inked in gall.

≈

One Fortuno Pelisson appears in Venetian court rolls,
Charged by a fourteenth-century landlord with poaching deer.
Though forced to write his name with "X," he could read
Paths scrawled through the forest by marten and fox.
Had he belonged to the class that signed itself with crests
His emblem would have shown a hoof caught in a snare.

The day of record he wanted vair, but when the fawn tripped
He made the best of it, selling its hide for parchment.
Yet he was cheeky and, through boasting, left his mark
By his sentence: *thrashed & sent six years to galley-work.*

≈

Sheep's handy, ox does in a pinch, goat serves well for parchment,
Though for the finest vellum he wants calfskin or the pelts of
    stillborn lambs.
And he's worked hares and wilder things: a brace of fawns,
Once, he thinned into the pages for a lady's thumb-sized Hours.

A slaked-lime bath, then stretching on the frame; his lunullum
Fresh-sharpened, whisking off both fat and fur; chalk pounce
Buffed in with pumice stone. At last, scraped again,
Each sheet veils light as a girl's ear does
When her back's to the fire. Truly, what eye'd prefer
Such surface limned, even with gold-leafed words?

≈

As you are now, so once was I.

Cowled skull and stooping spine
Mark the bones that worked with books.
From oak galls I ground our inks. I loved
Earth-smell in the oak woods.

As I am now, so thou shalt be.

When they laid me in the grave
My fingers wouldn't shed their skin.
Gall had tanned the palps so thick I'll hold
My earthly touch till judgment day.

≈

(marginal emblem, partially destroyed by fire)

Who am I? My order's name means marriage god and virgin-veil.
A nun of sorts, I have one kiss; when I give it away,
I die. You won't forget it easily. But leave me
A hollow log or lion's corpse and I'll sweeten it for you.
I'm the maid in the garden, while the maid in the garden
Drowses to my song. Though small, the libraries I build
House all the summer's hours. Poets envy
The honeyed tongue my sisters share, but our speech
Is all Zees. Kenning human, here's sugar on your lips.
My short name is your aim: To ---.

≈

He shows me where the fourteenth-century scrap peeks out

– Cookie jumped up, Suetonius fell, the parchment cracked,
Holy fuckoly! Then I saw this snippet of older manuscript
Sewn into the book's spine as a binding strip.

One legible word, red-lettered *holocausta*. An offering.
And the quires it holds, still tightly stitched
After the dog's harrowing, hint that the book's first body
Was wild, a deer perhaps, since we can see within each page
Faint veins left unbled when the pelt was stripped,
Tracery like antlers between branches in a beech forest.

≈

There was no word, in 1944, for it,
For what it seems has happened cyclically
Throughout recorded human history,
This thing between the tribes, this flaw
Of blood, perhaps inherent *in* our blood,
Inherited, this urge to kill the ones unlike ourselves.
No word, until a Polish linguist reaching back
Through Latin *genitalis* and the *genos* of the Greeks
To the mother-root that in the same century
Would bloom into the *genome,* named it.

≈

The Preacher's castigation *All is flawed*
Seems true, thank God: tests on finches suggest
A glitch on chromosome 7, where a winged
Helix box protein ages back changed
Its tune, turned birds to song and hominid
Throats toward speech. *Sing, cuccu, nu!*
                                    Cuccu,
Hymn this ghost in our cells' machine, skewed
Gene without whom my Pentecostal sister
Could neither praise the Word nor confess
In tongues, as the spirit moves her.

                    ≈

Slang's the tongue-fused bomb each generation
Lights to blow up its parents' house, especially
The bedroom. It's hard evolving louder expletives
Than they did, though. If *cock* began as a perversion
Used in oaths for God, *by coxbodikins* it soon
Shoved off that pious cowl and stood for other tricks!
Here's a rich evolutionary jism, or energy,
In hand. Whence cometh, say, that English *bird*
Blokes chirm about when they mean girl? Hatching from
An obscure egg, the term spreads its migratory

Wings across the Atlantic to feather her as *chick*.
It's possible, some linguists think, this bird corrupts
Bride, since rustling in its connotative tree's a woman
Willing to nest without a banded finger. But cock's
A bird as well, no? And boy, if you show me your
Uccello or *oiseau*, you're being fresh, with Romance
Vowels to lubricate. Which came first, goose or gander?
Saucy slang, I mouth your savor and in my saliva
Baptize you, tasting how a language craves
Spunk as well as the chrism of sacred names.

≈

Between etymology and entomology, the difference lies
In letters y and o and n. **Yes O**r **No?**

Biologists study the syntax of a bee's danced
Directions to a flower; the scholar traces a dozen languages'
DNA, words for parents, for the genitals and blood,
Back to reconstruct a vanished mother tongue.
Collectively the termites' intelligence builds its epic
Of mud; language is our hive. And when I die

The wasps will eat me and my paper words. But **O**,

Not **Y**et. This is my honeymoon above the earth.

≈

The dreaming keeper smokes the hive to stop the bees' stings.
The dreaming poacher masks his scent with urine from a doe.
The same knife that points the quill
Killed the dreaming crow.

One dreaming cell
Went astray and grew a tongue for speech.

The dreaming babe was born silent
When one rung fell.

Time yawns.

Then rings the bell.

III

Early

Atop a shanty near an open sewer
A rooster shouts.

                    A muezzin answers.

Here the tongues of church bells are
Replaced by human throats.

Fluency

Syria, 2009

Just returned from six months in the States,
Blinded by the burning screens of Google and Tweet
To body language on the street, I'm slow to understand the girl
Pointing at heaven, then at her ear and mouth,
Telling me God made her deaf and mute.

Shrewdly her bronze gaze appraises me.
I gesture at her stand and shrug. She flashes ten
Fingers, then ten again, showing what the lemons cost.
I nod. She bags a kilo, pinching her veil
Between her lips to cover her tattooed chin.

From my pocket I dredge a clutch of brassy coins.
Without taking her eyes off mine, she counts out twenty
Then shuts her hand quickly, making a cutting motion
Once to say *halas*, that's enough.
Veil wrinkling in her teeth, she grins at me.

Before universities, before
Embassies, the souk. Some palm-smoothed truth,
Warmed in this back and forth, will outlast all the information
I've spent a half year circulating.
I weigh my words here, learning what they're worth.

Bab

ب ا ب : a *door or gate*

First word of Arabic I learn to read
haltingly, and then try writing

باا baa
با baa

horned and hooved letters herded
leftward from the right.

≈

Scratch and start once more from scratch
illiterate again without a child's patience.

Here's gawkwardness I thought I'd lost, plus
the first forgotten attars of writing, fresh

pencil excelsior and the bleached paper's
whispery complaint against the rasping point.

≈

Lame as a kid's cursive
my sheepish figures
stray into the margins

با baa

browsing disconsolately
among trash and weeds.

≈

Bab

While my father read and smoked
I wrote my alphabet with tooth-brailled pencil

slowly on paper made for the learner.
Solid blue lines staggered with dashes

gave my grown-up B a pillow
on which to rest his dozy head, and taught

the ever-fidgeting toe of baby b
where she must stand to kick the *ball*.

When people talk about "the poetic line"

I remember how masterful I felt
sitting at the kitchen table with my father

having filled my pages edge to edge
with a family of big and little letters.

≈

Domesticate
this headstrong hoof and horn

baa ﺑ
baa ﺑ
baa ﺑ

through repetition.

ﺏ is the crucial consonant
for *bab* as well as *ibn,* "son."
Ibn is often shortened to *bin*
as in its Hebrew sibling, *ben.*

Bab

(The speakers may deny it
but language claims kin.)

≈

As my wrist builds muscle memory, it pulls
from memory's sinew a six-year-old self

cranking the wall-mounted sharpener's handle
slowly because she loved the cedar reek

eked off the pencil shavings in the trap, or pressing
pencil stems hard into the electric sharpener to draw

their hot, nervous shriek into her palm.
If it were silent writing time, she could control the room

through those nuanced registers of sound.
Back at her desk with a lancet lead, she'd send

the quiet class into screams of laughter
if she snagged the tip against the smallest

stitch of the paper's fiber and

– snap!

≈

How giddily I bleat as,
smooth on its hinges,
my little باب at last
unlatches!

Such unadulterated pleasure
when a locked door

Bab

opens on the tongue or
under your fingers!

≈

(– like learning to write your full given name
when a parent has been extravagant,

christening you in old-world batiste
syllables studded with end-of-the-alphabet

pearls he'd saved for your birth, as others
might hoard from the immigrant's dislocation

some gone century's too-ornate heirloom
silver in rouge-cloth for your trousseau.)

≈

Arabic has no letters for *V* or *P*
so my name is spelled approximately.

By the time my driver's license arrives
I read well enough not to recognize

the transliteration typed below
my awful-but-familiar photo

until, syllabizing all the way through,
I reach the patronymic *bint Claudio.*

My father's been dead for thirty years
but here he is, here he is

waiting for me in the cracked-open
door of a language he'd never spoken.

Bint, same root as *ibn. Daughter of.*
A word I translate here as love.

Arabesque

The heart of God is a honeycomb
           Where the sugar of starry flowers distills
Endlessly in perfumed cells
                     A cell for every soul that's lived

– or that, at least, is how I read the tendril
carved above me along the mosque's corbel,
though there are no human forms, of course;
only stone arabesques

           While the human heart is a smaller comb
Pressed from a daub of the same wax
                     Often sweetness drenches the ones
     Hiving its gold   but the human heart

– I'm startled then by the evening call to prayer
crackling across the roofs through a rusted speaker

Allahu' akbar   all melisma   then sustain

and for an instant on the horizon I see the moon
shiver as if it were the crescent over
a minaret reflected in moving water

but the street is filthy and the wind picks up again

                     The human heart's nectar is thin

Soft Power

for T.

ssssshshshshshshsssssshshshkhkhkkh

alarm   no, shortwave   frazzle, hiss

hiss of the weekly radio check, our safety
here at the far edge of the city tested

awake.

ssssshshshssssss T-bird, T-bird, this is Raptor, copy. Do you read?

I've felt you toss through dawn's call to prayer,
through the needle of widening light at the point
when white threads shine distinct from black.

Now on the desert's rim sun perches, spreading
wings of heat.

By voice, you recognize the new Marine from
Tucson.

T-bird here, Raptor. I read you loud and clear.

Now a shower, luxury in a region of drought.
A shave. A suit. And you depart for another day
reporting on trials in the criminal court.

≈

While I pass my morning in a poem's cool bosks
With a Bobolink for a Chorister

While I read in the meadows of solitude
    Where the mockingbird sounds his delicious gurgles

While I roam what I call the democracy of letters, accepting
    nothing which all cannot have their counterpart of on the
    same terms

≈

A hood of shadow must blind you as you step
from sun into the shuttered courthouse.
Then your pupils widen, letting in
signers of the Damascus Declaration,
eleven men shackled together in a cage.
Or a young lawyer arrested for blogging
critiques of the martial law, his charge
"weakening morale in time of war."
Activist Kurds. Members of the Muslim
Brotherhood. Old Marxists the regime
wants to shed. Your pupils widen on all
Adra prison will swallow.
Wives rock, fingering their beads.

And those who know you meet your eyes and tap
right hand to heart, showing they recognize
your eyes among the observers
allowed in from the embassies.

Your pupils, widening, sore.

When you leave the court, you carry
cages   babies   grains of barley
details you can't talk about with me

Against the bars of the cage women pressed babies
born since the men were arrested

stories I can only guess by counting
how many cigarettes you're smoking

Collected burnt grains of barley from his soup each night
in solitary, he says, until he had enough to make a pattern
filling his cell's floor

scraps chewed by silences

had to crouch in a corner
kept his sanity by making and unmaking
every day   for thirteen years   the same design

silences you'll translate into text I'll read
in the State Department's Human Rights Report.

≈

While I'm in the republic of poetry
Walking the old hills of Judea with the beautiful gentle god
by my side

≈

We've come to Syria for the wedding

Because this is not the old war

Because we catch more flies with honey

Because *if a state can make its power seem legitimate in the eyes*
of others

it will encounter less resistance to its wishes

Because *if its culture and ideology are attractive*
 others will more willingly follow

Because art's a golden band
and diplomacy a silken gown

We sugar
We sweet
We sticky

We thick syrup
as the glasses clink

≈

Saturday, our anniversary. Before dawn the Ramadan crier
whomps down the street with his drum: *Wake, O faithful! Prayer is*
 better than sleep!

A friend's teased you that our marriage is hardly proper
minus a ring. So with coffee you proffer – surprise! – a tiny package

ribboned with wit: "We've re-engaged the Syrians diplomatically;
it seems only proper I re-engage my wife." Bleariness blurs

to diamond tears. Ten years. You take my hand in yours
and band it. What silly laughter then in our little luxe nest!

Not till noon does a phone call pluck our calm.
A civil rights lawyer you admire is under arrest.

The two rings overlap, warm platinum
wedded to chill digital purr.

Soft Power

≈

We talk of doves and hawks
as if there were no other birds

Ramadan Kareem flicker the wee genie lamps over Ammar's shop.
My second cup of tea is drunk and with great show of head-
shakes and wrung hands   *my friend I'm too poor this week*

I've declined buying a carpet. Ammar has already sold me
the loveliest Qashqai in all the east; we're market cousins now;
I can't pass his shop without some chitchat and a sweet.

Below the portrait of Khaled Meshal I squat on "my" ottoman.
Ammar thanks me for the *New Yorker* I've brought.
"Roz Chast – oh, she splits my sides!" Then the muezzin cries,

breaking the fast. "Alhamdulillah!" Ammar studies the tray and,
delicately as he chooses idioms, selects a rosewater jelly.
He nibbles a corner "just to keep you company, my friend."

As if there were no doves or hawks
we talk of other birds

≈

Citizen of letters with her hot cumin tea
        Agonies are one of my changes of garments....
        I myself become the wounded person

Hot cumin tea and all the morning for reading
        My hurt turns livid upon me as I lean on a cane and
                observe

≈

At the new mall beside the old neighborhood
where Hezbollah slogans brighten broken walls
women in small clusters, scarved or baring
sunstroke blonded hair, buy Revlon lipstick,
Pixar movies, corn flakes from Battle Creek

You can feel soft power slipping in
through Billie's smoke-tranced croon,
film noir américain,
hip hop, Whitman

Power so soft it makes others want to be
plugged in to its source
simpatico   comrades   d'accord
without the need
(without the whisper)
of force

≈

Citizen of poetry I wander
            And sore must be the storm –

certain
            That could abash the little Bird

uncertain
            That kept so many warm –

≈

Studying Arabic in Washington while reading all we could on
      Guantánamo
including the DoD's online Gitmo album that made the compound

look like a Cuban Club Med – what, as the management types kept
    saying,
was our take away?

          We want
to send the inmates home but their own countries can't safely
    restrain them

            We have
no information about where they may have been in transit to our
    custody

                We mark
an arrow pointing toward Mecca on the floor of every cell
in fluorescent paint
so prisoners can pray in the dark

≈

bismillah ar-rahman ar-rahim   in the name of God most merciful
    and mild

≈

Awake in the land of the poetry of my land
    I am not to be denied....I compel....

    I am jetting the stuff of far more arrogant republics....

    Every room of the house do I fill with an armed force....

All morning
    The smallest Citizen that flies
    Is heartier than we

≈

A mourning dove settles on our balcony in Kafarsouseh.
I find her litter of twigs and needles

crotched among packing boxes we've never recycled.
On it, she's laid two alabaster stones. They help me weigh

your absorption in your work: you who miss so little
hadn't noticed she was here.

She grows calm with me coming out to watch her.
Some mornings when my thoughts are less

coherent than blowing sand
I just stand, studying the colors of her neck.

Wide from the dark inside, my pupils take
long seconds of daylight to narrow

on fired lilac, emerald gray.
A hot, gassy blue.

≈

Raptor here, T-Bird. T-bird, do you copy?

≈

Once, you told me, at home, walking into the woods
an hour before the dawn, the oaks

were alive with owls calling back and forth.
A pair of great wings dropped with that barely audible

creak of air through its plumes and hung a few seconds
just above your head. Uncertain, you said,

if you were threat
or food.

Wind

called "the fifty" because it can blow that many days

Low through every crack
The khamsin moans, then rises to a howl
Loud enough to muffle the shabab
Gunning their motorcycle
Smokily in circles round the park.
By noon, they've given up.
Sand fills the air and the sun goes dark.

No walk to the souk, then. No run.
Restless, I soak chickpeas, read recipes
I know I'll never make, fritter half the afternoon
Away between half-
Interesting books. Where's that self, at home every
Place she lands and landing always on her feet?
This wind has thrown her compass off.

When Napoleon met this wind
Coursing up the Nile on his campaign
To liberate the Orient,
It was France's first foray
Eastward since the last Crusade.
Learning its name's meaning, he thought *but can they
Really count that high?* That was an underestimate.

His plans went south. A canal across the Suez?
Non. Boulevards? Hospitals?
A new system of weight and measure?
Non. Non. They found the Rosetta Stone (and took it),
Then left occupying soldiers
Cursing untranslatably in their chasseur-blue jackets.
Then those withdrew. Then civil war.

There's a lull in the roar near five.
I shut my book and duck out to the mall for milk, but I've
No sooner rounded the corner
Than I'm pinned against a wall by blasts
Scouring the condo tower.
Between its teeth the furious desert grinds my face,
Whipping my hair into viperous

Coils that slash the tissues
I'm having a sheol of a job
Holding tight against my mouth and nose.
Can a wind *hate* you? I suppose I'm being silly.
A passing girl flicks me
A look of sympathy
Through the squints in her niqab.

Old City

Singed sheep's heads in pyramids
Teeth still grassy glazy eyes
Gazing at their own entrails
Seeping off the scales

Near the pelts of Asian wolves
Silver flags strung
From hooks spiking the rotting
Metal air with musk

This is the only way, I think, the strong lie down beside the weak.

No. Don't go there.
Brooding never does you any good.
Walk through the souk instead.

Cardamom   sumac   saffron   rose petal
Apricot paste   sesame crackle

Candles shaped like the hand of Fatima
God's eye in the palm and a pink wick
Poking from each henna'd fingertip

Bricks of olive oil soap   then more
Soap bricks stacked in larded courses
Packed like turrets buttressing the stalls

The walk itself a cleansing ritual.

Bijouterie of olive shops
Rusting drums heaped with gray
Green   glassy-brown   onyx

Old City

Scions of the branch the dove
Carried back to Noah's hand

The walk itself a cleansing ritual.

Until it starts to rain.

Inside a khan I shelter with three pubescent boys.

Min win entum?
Min Iraq.

They've set down their cardboard trays of gum.

Each stands   lifting one bare foot
Then the other up to warm
Over a fire in a ruined olive drum.

Lot's Wife

Dead Sea, Jordan, 2009

A man with a camera,
Bikinied women sipping wine,
And a child loudly refusing his *dejeuner*
Cure in brine
On the mineral crust of the hotel beach

When blasts begin,
Low, muffled first by distance,
Percussive then as they explode
Closer, insistent,
Till the ice is knock-kneed in every glass.

The man snaps pictures.
Women point and crowd together.
Wailing, the boy abandons his gothic
Moat and tower.
Our drinks sweat, forgotten.

Only the bow-tied
Palestinians bussing our empties
Seem indifferent to the smoke off what
We realize slowly
Is practice on the opposite bank.

"Lot's Wife,"
They call that pillar of salt by the road.
She faces west, not back but across the water
Thick as blood
Where nothing lives but bitterness.

The King's Baths

Hammam al-Malik, Damascus, built 985 A.D.

for Tracy and Samuel

Day and night beneath caravansary stars
When he's a man, Samuel will travel his dreams
Seeking the echoing rooms of the hammam
Where,
When he was four, he scooped water from a pool
Carved in the ablaq floor
While in a circle above him steamed
Globes spiced with every earthly color:
The breasts a dozen diplomats and aid workers
Carried before them to Syria,
Along with his mother's.

Splashing, water pistols, soap in the eyes.
Then supper spread banquet-style
Along a low table as the apple smoke of narghile
Blued the air into an orchard
Curling perfumed leaves up toward the dome. And Samuel –
Having launched his loofah like Saladin's
Mangonel against the infidel
Hordes at the Battle of Hattin
Again at the Danish Red Cross Director's head
Before being démarched
And disarmed long enough to share
Her bowls of hummus and za'atar –
Flung himself across his mom and fell
Asleep in the folds of her towel

So he never saw
The hammam ladies drape
Themselves in black jilbab and sweep
Escaping wings of hair back into plaits
Tightly caged with clips beneath hijab,

Or his mother's colleagues swap
Turkish-terry robes for the limp
Damp skins of hose and locker-
Wrinkled business clothes.

Cold stars woke him.

Goodbyes rose spiraling
Up alleys from the women
Leaving the harem to resume
Once more the homely equilib-
Rium
Between ceding ground and strategic shows of power,
The tact and
Tactics for prevailing
Diplomatically over
Any state governed
By children
Or kings.

Unbeliever's Prayer

"…and gardens with streams of water where they will abide forever."
– Al Qur'ān 3:136

for Julia Wickham

O Merciful,
Your Prophet says perfumes of running water await the believer in
    Paradise.
Cool streams where jasmine blossoms float will bathe the faithful
    feet.
Thick with dates, palm fronds will drip
Syrups to sweeten his tongue
Till he forgets all lies, all thirst.
At night, the angels' torches hang above the olive trees,
Lighting the garden whose music is
Part bulbul and part oud.

It sounds very good.

But, Compassionate, will you grant to one
Who cannot fit her soul through the eye of a needle
– A stranger, yet grateful for your hospitality –
Leave to camp outside your gate?
For my eyes and ears are wealthy.
Wealthy are my lips.
And if such richness cannot join the pure
Passing through your garden's walls,
Will your Benevolence allow me for company
Your homeliest daughter, the camel?

Allow me the obstinate one who, tapped by her drover's cane
Commanding her to couch, bellows
Before collapsing front end first to her parchment knees,
Who groans like a slit waterskin and vomits
Cud dense as half-cooked bulgur over her drover's heels.

She is justifiably aloof: alone
Among all creatures including men
Who praise your ninety-nine names
She knows your final, hundredth, name.

She smells like the birth of the world:
Iron and salts, ammonia and calcium,
Urine evaporating off sandstone in the heat.

From her shoulders her felted pelt hangs, carded by the wind
Into Bedouin patterns against the evil eye.
The thickets in the wadis of her ears
Have trapped grains of the Sahara blown north
On every storm since she was calved.

Peevish, she has torn with jaws
Only half-toothed yet strong as a djinn
In one swift grab a man's kneecap from his leg.
But offered a chocolate biscuit from a sweaty palm
She drops her eyelashes and presses
Her split top lip, like two adroit fingers
Opposed by her lower lip's thumb,
Gently into the cup of the giver's hand,
Not missing a crumb.

Her bristled tongue is stiffer than her hooves.
Half-stuffed leather cushions, they flatten at each step to grip
Sands of the peninsula and Levant
That roast any lingering moisture from the air,
And from the bodies of all traveling there,
And surely are what your Prophet must be picturing
Every time he mentions hell.

Across them she can travel a week without water,
Or only brackish water

Lifted in rancid goatskins from stinking wells,
Or water so salt it scorches the human throat.

There are perfumed streams in Paradise, they say.

But I know my place.

Give me leave, Merciful, to rest
Outside your garden's gate
With one loved by parched souls for her endurance
So ample that, if that is all there is,
She makes a feast of thorns.

Damascened

for Wael and Maysoon

Moon's sliver
Crook't in the east –
A fertile crescent?

Or scimitar
Over necks
Bent in prayer?

> When we arrived,
> You revealed
> Nerves steeled
> To knive's blades
> With inlaid alloys
> Damascened,
> Hardened, hammered,
> Tempered, sharpened,
> Oriented like pearls
> Of water, oiled.

>> Slowly then,
>> You wove us in.
>> Days took on
>> Damask silk's
>> Tensile fall.
>> How fragile these
>> Creature-spun
>> Fibers feel,
>> Yet they remain
>> Stronger still
>> When pulled upon
>> In memory
>> Than same-gauge
>> Threads of steel.

Pulled away,
Our eyes ache
With your hopes,
Crushed beneath
Too great
A weight of sights.

But so it was
When mortar stones
Expelled attars
From the rose.

Cooled, distilled,
And veiled from light
In clay jars
At Ugarit,
That rich perfume
Soothed the callous
Hands of kings
Before the days
Of Abraham,
Before those hands,
Filled with fire,
Fell in fire.

Above the sand
Stars circled
Centuries.

Then, discovery.
Ancient jars'
Seals were breached,
Pitch cracked
From corked necks
– And rare fumes

Damascened

Filled the lab's
Air with scent
Faint but fine
From Damask Rose
Blossoms whose
Ghost the stone
Intensified,

Essences
Lasting out
The grind's press
Before out-
Lasting time.

Counted on a String of Beads

"God preserve you"

Owl-spectacled falafel vendor near the Mosque of Sinan Pasha who layered mint leaves densely as pages in my sandwich, *Allah yehmeek*.

Pimply boy hawking mulberry juice under the overpass on the highway to Jordan, *Allah yehmeek*.

G., certainly queer, for unraveling a souk's-worth of scarves and modeling them for me, *Allah yehmeek* to you and all your secrets.

And *Allah yehmeek* to you, Bassam, weaving Damask silk at Madrasa Selimiye, who showed me how antique cards brailled with holes, like those I used to "sew" with a shoelace when I was little, control the loom's pattern of threads.

Shy clerk who helped me weasel my head into a hijab, *Allah yehmeek*. You apologized so abjectly for touching my hair.

White kittens I fed but never brought home from the park in Kafarsouseh, *Allah yehmeekoum*.

Ameed, *Allah yehmeek*. I'm sitting next to the trunk you carved, cypress wood inlaid with a mother-of-pearl tree-of-life.

Iraqi Anna who would walk to our apartment for a glass of water, *Allah yehmeeki*. *Allah yehmeekoum*, too, to your deported sons.

Allah yehmeekoum and *Yevarechecha Hashem Veyishmerecha* to the last rabbi and his sister, not afraid to show us the locked temple and score of Torahs the departing Jews were forced to leave behind.

Allah yehmeek, Joe Sarki, thank you for making my wedding ring.

It helps me pass as a respectable woman. We hear you made it safely to Beirut.

Allah yehmeek, Mazen, arrested February 16 at the newspaper office and not seen since. Reporters Without Borders says you've been tortured and may be sentenced to death. I read this online and had no idea what to do except walk into the garden and pick clean lavender sprigs to put in the copper bowl you gave us at W.'s party.

Ancient ageless Fatti, *Allah yehmeeki*. Have you been able to recite "No Coward Soul Is Mine" with your vowels oval as wren's eggs at Jane Digby's grave this year?

Skinny Palestinian kid always riding your too-big-bicycle and racking yourself in the parking lot near the convenience store, *Allah yehmeekoum* to you and your family.

Ladies crown-to-ankle veiled with full niqab but wearing sneakers, who powerwalked around the block each morning, *Allah yehmeekoum*.

Allah yehmeek, Abd. When you wrote last month that you were in danger and asked if I could get you a visa, I'm so very very sorry I was so molar-grindingly helpless.

Allah yehmeekoum, Shia girls just arrived from Tehran who shared your rosewater candy.

Allah yehmeekoum, Kurdish waiters waiting for a homeland at Café Set as-Shem.

To all the devout who refused to shake my hand but bowed heads and tapped right hands to hearts, *Allah yehmeekoum*.

Allah yehmeekoum, waterwheels of Hama and stuffed carrots of Homs.

Allah yehmeekoum, five generations of Armenian goldsmiths in Aleppo. I visit the burned souk in my dreams.

Allah yehmeek, Mustapha. I will never forget the chicken with garlic your friend grilled for us behind the crusader castle. What wind on the ramparts! Remember how hot it was that day in Tartous?

May I be excused now for craving a drink and asking Allah to watch over awful Barada beer?

And its stinking namesake river?

And the Phoenician ghosts of Amrit and Ugarit, where our feet crunched Bronze-age potsherds lying among the stones?

Allah yehmeekoum, pinched old men who didn't like women smoking hookah at Nowfara Coffee Shop. I was so happy adding my blue apple exhalations to your cloud.

Ammar, *Allah yehmeek, yehmeek*. I'm waiting to finish our argument. I still have your book.

Late

Kharoof, kharoofain, kharaweef,
The single, the dual, the many.

Sleepless while the clock ticks
I still count sheep in Arabic.

IV

The Monongahela Book of Hours

Pennsylvania

A page to hold this place. Illuminations sharp
Enough to catch the river's pitch, canoe's

Clip around a rock, the redwing's dive above
Stove-in banks of smoking trash, dark earth's plunge

To underworlds where men still crouch to free
The stone whose flesh is flame, whose bone

Is time, whose ghostly ash the rains
Wash down into the pool from which,

Blue in the owl-annotated woods past town
At dawn, deer pick their way to drink.

≈

Spectral fog along a mountain interstate some-
Place between the solid world we left and these
Gauzed altitudes where we have come to live,

A convoy of trucks ahead so it's not until we nearly drive
Right through them that I heel the brake and, swerving,
Miss a mother goose parading her unfledged flock
Across the median and straight into our lane.

We miss, but in the mirror watch the rigs behind
Bear down and scatter them as easily as leaves,
As feathers, into the oncoming lights.

≈

Small towns in mining country. Everyone seems a little
Off somehow, the damage often clear but slight.
Missing fingers, a limp. In others, deeper harm emerges
From a slack mouth or gaze trained on sights beyond.
Christian fellowship is advertised, though churches
Outnumber visible occupants.
                              When we park and walk
In, the few stare like we came from the moon
And all our own oddness quivers up coldly magnetized,
The way a vein of iron oxide threaded through
A rock will make a compass needle shake.

≈

Dog walk. Ahead the path grows over, lightly breeze-blown,
Margins illuminated by the trembling hand of a novice
Monk. Mining kills the water, but horror vacui
Drives nature still, as it drove rows of cowled shoulders
Bent in the scriptorium to fill the vellum's flank
With hatchings of azure and orpiment.

For Matins, paint the redwing blackbirds'
Epaulets ablaze in preened display, the marsh-side trees
A loggia from which the flocking aristocracy
Drop alms of song onto your path.

≈

First day of hunting season? Show a movie, advises my chair. *Half*
    your kids
Won't be there. Meanwhile, some ancient protein in Tony's DNA,
Long-couched, flares its nostrils at the cave's mouth and sniffs the
    air.
Borrowed, an uncle's camo jacket. Pants patterned in Leafy Oak
Breakup, bought. For masking human scent, urine from an estrous
    doe –
Capric, armpit-rich, almost a burn on the back of the tongue,
Purchased under the brand name *Still Steamin'*. Topo maps. Tarp.
His father's bow, restrung, waiting in a case the same size as
His guitar. And the hi-tech arrow points he packs the night before,
Designed to burst on impact into five-bladed stars.

≈

Hiroshige, a minor bureaucrat in the shogun's retinue,
Charged with delivering a gift horse to the emperor,
Traveled the Tokaido road in 1832, sketching views
He later printed from woodblocks – simple images
Of lumbermen guiding their logs along the river
Or tax collectors, stopped at the Futagawa teahouse,
Entertained by geishas. His prints translate the world
To floating dream with little fuss. Pilgrims ford streams
With the aid of loinclothed bearers, and women hold parasols
Half-shut to shelter their horsehair wigs from snow.

≈

In early snow a hunter knelt by the carcass
Of a whitetail buck and looked again into its barely-
Clouded eye. What he watched receding in the pupil

That had locked on his and held him still a full
Three beats before he loosed the arrow, he would not tell.
Now the deer was a winter's meat.

When he came from cleaning it to warm his hands
And kissed me, I couldn't recognize his smell.
Like the bride in the folktale, I woke to find

I had married the forest, married the deer.

≈

And if there were a Hiroshige of the mill towns?
The visions closest to his clarity are the postcards one student
Brings me from an antiques mall, printed when tourists came
Frequently enough to warrant souvenirs of local sights. So I own
Snapshots of Mingo Bridge and Monongahela,
Tinted in aqueous pastel. The block prints are timeless;
Even if the artist never saw such scenes, his images
Conjure an eternal world. But photographs are full of time.
Merciless smiling shadows of the lost, the last Mill Ball Team
Before Pittsburgh fell to the flood of Japanese steel.

≈

Oxidized kiln skins. Quanta of junked glass.
How many autumns of sumac rusting

Beside the tipple and the strip mall's buckled parking lot
Before this halflife, also, decays?

Mine shut. Residents gone. For thirty years
Glance seams below the town have burned,

Sulfur venting through rents in the tar,
Roads cracking and sunk in this Flegrea where

Steel-hooved industry breached the crust
Dividing upper world from under.

≈

[Quecreek mine accident, 2002]

Could you die each day and descend to that black realm
Borne under on the bier of the mantrip?
And there eat oily jewels of sunlight
Trapped in trees that fossilized to coal?

These are the negatives of stars, for which
Men give their breath.

Waiting in the air above
The flooded mine, imagination is an awful tool.

Rise Lazarus, rise Christus, rise
As in old myths the daughter returns and life
Blooms from under the earth in a rush of water.

≈

After single-point perspective, I want omniscient sight.

Not just the news camera's flash outside a drowned shaft,
But the crush of the miner's pick breaching
The unmapped well, and water's vision winking out his light.

What a coal seam sees with its legion black eyes.

The merchants, matrons, dogs, and gladiators buried at Pompeii
Left only their ash-filled hollows.

But painted near them on a tufa wall
The goddess Flora turns, Flegrea

Greening again below her heel.

≈

[Photo, 1904]

    White man in blackface
Of coal. Among a blackface crew. A mile below surfaces where he

    Might elbow a *nigger* off
Sidewalks. Or not? Too new yet to muscle into his stratum in the
    shifting

    Tectonics of *hunkies, dagoes, kikes?* Bodies
Steeraged from cabbage-water towns where mustaches were the
    only

    Flourishing concern. No middle passage but slops, rats
Eating the straps off the baby's shoes. All cats look the same in the
    dark

Pit, the newcomer says in his
Tongue that sounds to the shift crew like a cat being skinned.

≈

Artless demi-creature, at sixteen I'd sport with boys
Then plump my pillows, smooth the shamefaced teddy bears.

Now when my students file in wearing tee-shirts printed with
    kittens
Or Pooh clutching his honeypot,

Cropped to bare their navel rings, they evoke that last
Grasp at girlhood, that threshold where

Toothy blowjobs overlap homesick devotion to toys.
How old was Flora when the dark god tore her

From her meadow? The students chatter, flutter, settle, turning
Their cell phones off and their pages to Ovid.

≈

Long before lending its name to the bug we're warned can now
    be *weaponized*

Before Pittsburgh's reek made it *hell with the lid off* (though some
    locals joked

The artificial darkness spared them from sun's glare)   When
    airborne

Rainborne sulfurs hadn't licked holes in the marble acanthus on
    libraries

Yet-to-be-endowed by Carnegie and Frick   Earlier than railways

Giving Londoners the habit of carrying black umbrellas against its
soot

Before Star Chamber convened to hear complaints against *the
dregs of many counties*

Daillie drunkards flooding Newcastle to work the mines   Or the
narrow flues

Demanding chimney sweeps no bigger than a child   Before
canaries

Before pit ponies   Before pits   When the Dance of Death had
not yet kicked

High its heels through Restoration smog (its steps: *Piles, Planet,
Rising*

Of the lights, one ailment simply called *Mother,* all worsened by

Smoaky air where babes reeled and spun and *perisht fast)*   Earlier
than

The London medico who wrote of buboes swelling hot until

Like carbuncles of sea-coal they wept necrotic matter   Even
before

The Venerable Bede observed the fume of fired *jet-stones* noxious

And useful for routing snakes   Ovid's fellows prized coal's
scintilla

When faceted and set with gems as on this anthracite medallion

Worn for fertile marriage by a girl, look, no older

Than you, my dears, whose eyes in her funeral portrait burn.

≈

Some Adam, hopeful or huckstering or ironic,
Seeing hills behind the tipple smoked in greenery,
Named this patch town *Muse*. Its economy
Leans today on auto shops and taxidermy.

All, sayeth the Lord on the Baptist church marquee, *is vanity.*

If you see rainbows in your water glass, don't drink,
Our neighbor warns. *Your well's drawing gasoline.*
On Sundays in service the faithful forsake this place
For Beulah Land, but love it, swallow its poison,

And won't leave it willingly for any place but heaven.

≈

Grief in its local dress is piercing yet picturesque.
Here lies *Zarinda Fainter, Young Mother*,
And at her side five miniature blank slates. One by one
Unhoused too soon, or all erased in a sole fell swoop?
A winged death's-head wipes clean her name.

Often the stones say so little that I'm drawn
By silence to author their stories. In our second year,
I learn to gather morels by the bed of my best tragedy,
The minister's brontophobic daughter who,
Fleeing raindrops, fell down a well and drowned.

≈

To live where beauty batters your heart while poverties
Bruise your mind, you must… what? From books I mined

No answer. So, to stop asking, I ran, hammering my bones
Each night against the hills. Caterpillars tented the sumacs

Like silicotic lungs and my own breath burned from climbing
Above pleated rows of houses aproned by church yards

Sewn with the small gray pockets of graves. We're all
Compressing into coal. Once I'd thought great weight

Packed coal to diamond. But I was wrong. It was a common
Stone I was hardening into as the months bore down.

≈

[Henry Clay Frick, 1849-1919]

Born in the springhouse footing his grandfather's land,
This measle wouldn't have survived a week
Without his nurse's mustard poultice on his belly
Every time he screeched. Reaching boyhood, he thrived
On hot dreams of doubling the old man's wealth.

On cold cash borrowed against his father's farm,
He bought his first coal field. Barely of age, he bartered
His health and almost lost, but savored challenge,
Made risk his meat. Learned not to take *no* for an answer.
Married. Built a manor. Buried his favorite daughter.

≈

[1862]

In my grandfather's house there are many mansions
And an ottoman with legs cut from a deer.
Down to cloven hooves the ankles spindle.
It crouches, a satyr's cushion waiting to scamper,
When he whistles, to his heel. On it

I hunch, reading Thucydides. *Of gods we believe*
And of men we know – the Athenian
Boldness swells my throat – *their nature decrees*
Wherever they can rule, they will. I rule grandfather,
And his dogs spread suppliant bellies at my feet.

≈

Figures are two things he understands,
Drawings of the body and arithmetic.
He marries them on his money
Where a gleaning woman and a miner with a pick
Work above the legend

> *H.C. FRICK & COMPANY*
> *DUE BEARER   ONE DOLLAR*
> *IN GOODS*
>
> *AT OUR STORE*
> *BROADFORD, 1874*

The scrip's green grays the bearer's hand.

≈

[Alexander Berkman, anarchist]

My tongue is raw, but like Caliban I've learned
The master's language well enough to curse.

Damned if we'll die the servants of a king
Bloated on his throne of smoke; damned if we'll mine
His empire, crouched below the earth to pluck
These sulfurous nuts he roasts at night.

He boasts of freeing sunlight, trapped inside each fossil tree
Whose leaves drank in the day before it turned to stone.

Flame, he says, is that spirit's jubilation.

I'll kill him when we're alone.

≈

[July 6, 1892: The Homestead Strike]

The river at Pittsburgh seemed to Berkman
A starved worker stretching his arms toward monsters
Belching fire into the giant hive.

So Frick, the monster-king, must die.

But all Berkman's sense of justice – plus three bullets,
Much stabbing, and a bomb clenched in his teeth – failed.

While the weeping anarchist was led from the office
Frick dabbed his wounds and went on signing deeds.

Shoot to kill, Frick ordered strikebreakers. And thrived,
Buying mines and European art the city's soot attacked.

≈

[Book of Hours calendar page, 15th c., Frick Collection]

Illustrating March, two men have worked their arms stiff
Swinging pruning hooks for six centuries in this
Vineyard on a hill. They cannot read the book
Where the painter has made them pastoral marginalia
For a parade of nobles entering the season,
Page left. An ounce of the powdered lapis bluing
The constellations above them is rarer, nearly,
Than peace. The painter, not knowing he had only half
A zodiac left until plague felled him, spent hours picking out
The men's limbs in lampblack with a licked brush.

≈

[The Homestead Works, 1881-1986]

Rumor says, when a man fell into a ladle of molten steel
The foreman ordered that ingot set in a corner of the yard.

Later when they got busy again, he'd have it reheated,
Rolled, and shipped. Homestead bodies hardened into beams.
Beams girded the country. From the Chrysler Building
To the bridge at Oakland Bay, how many Homestead hours
Built the twentieth century?
                              Their tale-tall hero was a mule like them:
Joe Magarac, big as a smokestack, drank hot metal for soup
After squeezing rail through his fingers. To save the failing works
He fired himself to vapor tears in the Bessemer furnace.

≈

Sadness, a gently purgatorial Sunday sadness.
Is it because there's no mail to distract me
From my surroundings or myself? From meditating
Whether our sweet neighbor's vision of how we'll pass
Eternity at the picnic of evangelical afterlife
Counts as penance when I'm obliged to listen?

Let the saved greet their own salvation.
The church-goers in church. The grass-goers
Chewing a blade as they lie on their backs,
So still a hawk circles, considering.

≈

Look, you haven't been exiled here, so don't get all sniffy,
Professor. Sure, Ovid's Rome seems more familiar,

His Tomis even, where the poet finally admits,
Writing in their barbaric tongue, that he's grown fond

Of the natives. But home is where your work is, and if it comes
Graced by a plate of funnel cake, say *thank you*.

Get your nose out of the book awhile. You'll never quite fit,
But you can learn to paddle a canoe, spot deer in a stand of brush,

And when you turn venison into good red sauce, the neighbors
Take seconds and see you're not a total loss.

≈

Pumiced by dust, a miner's lungs are frailer
Than the antique player piano rolls I find
Coffined in our Victorian parlor's closet. Unscrolled,
"The Monongahela Nocturne" spreads its stigmata
Of notes. Breaker boys dividing culm from coal
Barehanded in the mills the year our house was built
Suffered *red tips* when sulfur gnawed their fingers raw.
My fingers trace where the cylinder bit
Each punched hole, translating, triggering the piano's
Proper keys.
         So emptiness began this song.

≈

Far above our earthly woods, our earthly waters,
Springs the river Eridanus from Achernar, star
Of the first magnitude. Then heaven's flume of tears
Trickles north to where I drink it, iced,
From my telescope's glass. In its shallows,
Splashed by his hounds, Orion dabbles his hucklebones.

Orion the Hunter, the ancients named him. But here
Winter dark is no game. It's a coal seam through rock.
So I call him *Orion the Miner*, pick and shovel in hand,
The three stars at his belt a hammer, a pail, a lamp.

≈

The first temple was a grove of trees
Hung with sacrificial skulls. The gods praised there were beautiful
And wild, and often took the form of animals.

Our neighbor never mentioned this.
But a pair of mounted turkey cocks, an elk's tooth-crenelated
Lower jaw, and a twelve-point whitetail rack
Crammed the bedroom where he died.

Silent, he was welcomed back to the church.

After the funeral we built a fire in his sodden field,
Sending his kills to honor him in smoke.

≈

[whispered into smoke]

Overhead the caravansaries of stars
Light their revolving lamps to welcome you
As they greeted your teacher, Ptolemy.

The spring Crab scuttles the ecliptic west,
Stretching a claw to the Water Serpent's head.
In its belly, the Beehive Cluster hums with young
Stars seeded from hydrogen and dust.
                                        You loved
Insisting your DNA was engineered like that,
In space, and we knew the fields were just
Your pied-à-terre, the air your truer habitat.

≈

Before the leaves flesh out in spring, a hunter follows
Deer trails lacing the woods, pokes at scat, scratches
At scrapes, daily leans a few more blowdown limbs together
For a blind.
          Days lengthen.
Chlorophyll pulls sunlight into stems.
New vines tendril over, then blanket the blind.

At dusk on the meadow's edge a doe raises her head
From rampant green to watch a passing fox.

Chill on lengthening grass, the moon makes the hunter
Impatient for dawns of frost, the owl's call.

≈

Monongahela, my river *where bluffs fall down to the water,*
Though King Coal's steamed west and steel has folded,
You're still too freighted with commerce to canoe.

But you may school us yet in metamorphoses, for all
Your northward-flowing length, where once Flegrean toxic
Waters flamed, your banks this summer blaze green.

Below the locks we paddle your tributary.

When a kingfisher dives, Tony masters his surprise, tucks us
Neatly into an eddy turn to watch its plummeting refrain,
And as we hang mid-stream the redwings clamor on the bank.

≈

Lungs are frailer, too, than a Book of Hours' vellum page
Given its tooth for ink six hundred years ago
With a pounce of ashes. *Vita brevis,*

The calf bawled in the yard. The birds in the bush
Rustled till their limed feet burned, their bones
Charred and ground to whiten the calf's singed hide.

The monks' calligraphy, Flora frescoed on the villa walls,
Aquarelles of the river's span at night below
A multitude of stars. How sharply they shine, *ars longa, ars*

Longa, painted fires lighting the painted water.

≈

Not of the diamond's water, this flame.
Not rich, not pure, not rare.

A common stone, burning, by which I've lived.
A sulfured smutch, a sputtering match.

Not diamond, but ancient
Sunlight through a leaf

Unsheathed from rock by the bare
Fingers of a boy.

Truth is, these are his bones.

I've gnawed them to a skeleton of song.

≈

["The Monongahela Nocturne"]

Indian Summer burned two weeks before the weather
Finally turned, and tonight acorns drop, popping, in fog. Now
   rain
Moves over; oaks rattle their leaves in a slaking that brings
Water's course to the schoolyard and the narrow glen
Bedded with whitetails, to the road, the track, the shotgun
Shacks, to the pool of tailings dabbled by ducks,

And when it leaves us at midnight, it leaves rinsed stars
Trembling as notes in the nocturne: *Fire above me,*
Fire below, fire in all four quarters, anthracite
Night, and carbon the body of miners.

V

Human Field

Now it snows, invisible air given
        A ghost's body by motes
Fleet as the fireflies' sexual isotopes

        Igniting the meadow with little half-lives,
But colder. A starling flock, disrupted,
        Ascends and circles twice in loose

Precision, high enough to seem the very
        Negative of snow: emphatic, demanding,
Warm flesh below the feather, though their bones

        Are hollow and their bivalve hearts
Lighter than a sanded clam shell
        Or the whitest pearl.

        Winter's revenant
Invites you into it, and there you lie
        While the bleached sheet, accumulating,

Translates you to an angel in a solitary bed.
        Beat your wings to leave your signature,
Sole mark on the virgin manuscript.

        Or, still now, the figure weeping on a tomb.

What are you hiding from, in a body of snow?

        A touch and it melts on your finger.

Because this is not your element, no matter
        How long you lie, unblinking, to watch it
Falling from a bloodless sky,

        Faster now, faster, till all the field is white.

Songs for the Boisterous Month

Anglo Saxon "Hlyd-Monath," March

for Karen Holmberg

These dull, doggish,
Cloud-drowned dawns,
The sluggard brain
Drugs the body to lie abed.
My circadian chemical
Clockwork waits, tickless,
For lighter fingers
To wind it.

Till one morning in early March
(Though each year
I forget and wake
Shocked in the suddenly
Lively dark) all the birds are
Riotously back.
The eaves give shelter
And their wicker arch-
Itecture starts as the each-
Day-quicker-
Receding hour
Before light, *your*
Hour, leads us by ear
Toward summer –

≈

The first to toss   its plum cockade to the wind's briskly
  Martial riffle,   this violet's scent's so delicate
It can't be sensed   unless the thumbnail shako-plume's
  Ensconced in some   small vial that concentrates its smell.
    (An odor scrawls   its signature illegibly
      Till chemicals   triggered by humidity

```
      Attach their cells        along receptors in your nasal
        Membrane walls.)          What a fine distillery
       A shot glass makes,       trapping faint perfume within
        A swig of air.         Knock back this draught of dense-
   Compacted scent:        along long chains of synapses
      The violet's liquor      stings, warming up your insect
       Brain, whose wings,        all winter folded snug against
        The numbing cold, unfurl and *lo!* – the insect sings.
```

≈

A turncoat night brings winter back.
The crocus on the slope is glassed in ice.

≈

Snows come down
But do not stick to boughs that drip
Glassy paillettes from each tip.

A cardinal's flown
From brambles where his startling cap
Prophecies their rising sap

Across the lawn.
Pecking seed from a feeder cup,
He showers more than he picks up

Till seed lies strewn
Below his swinging perch. His crop
Swells like a silk cravat. One hop –

He's gone.

≈

First moon of the Roman calendar.
Its luster limns each naked twig, so the branch
Before its disk appears
The net some bronze-clad shield is fished
Up dripping from the river in.

≈

New bark on her tongue, the doe
Shifts restlessly in snow, and the buck
Lays down his ragged crown of thorns.

≈

A late spring snowfall blurs the half-blown buds.
Day tucks its eye below the woods' wing.

My path through the meadow is blank,
The hiss of my skis a prompt:

What is your truest attribute?   Stubbornness.
What is its root?   My will.

I am a will
Making its own way, slowly, on skis.

I'm dusk's quill, the nib where it presses
Twin lines of smoke-blue signature against the snow.

To Certain Students

On all the days I shut my door to light,
All the nights I turned my mind from sleep

While snow fell, filling the space between the trees
Till dawn ran its iron needle through the east,

In order to read the scribblings of your compeers,
Illiterate to what Martian sense they made

And mourning my marginalia's failure to move them,
You were what drew me from stupor at the new day's bell.

You with your pink hair and broken heart.
You with your knived smile. You who tried to quit

Pre-law for poetry ("my parents will kill me").
You the philosopher king. You who saw Orpheus

Alone at the bar and got him to follow you home. You
Green things, whose songs could move the oldest tree to tears.

Suspect

A week in January warm as this
Has the environmentalists

Shaking heads; and the redbud, now
Reckless, blushes, though snow

Forecasted in the coming days
Will surely chasten it. Why,

Knowing chlorofluorocarbons
Kindled this week's bright blazons,

Are we lightened? Over the college lawn
Laughter wafts from bodies strewn

Beside a Frisbee game, whose players
Shed their winter layers and use

Cast-off coats to mark the goal.
Haven't we been schooled?

How suspect a chemical
Is happiness, when the sun's unveiled eye all

Evidence shows we should fear
Still makes us bask in its splendor.

Where the Arrows Fell

At the upturns of your grin, the red beard
     This year's begun threading itself with white.
  "Each agéd hair a gift" – kiss – "from you."
    You're joking, mostly. But in some deeper sense
It's true: we're married now, you've vowed
     Your life and all your coming years to me.
   Whatever other nuptial rites we cast out

    As too tribal, not our style (the virgin
Gown, the given girl, the fertility-
     Provoking garter), we assume we'll weather
  Through the turning hairs, or their decline,
    Together. And if we're successful, one of us,
Barring some unlikely twinned demise,
     Must end without the other. That's why

  I cried before our rustled-up, gum-
    Chewing justice who kept calling you "Andy"
By mistake. You thought it was my normal mild
     Hysteria, mixed with trying not to laugh.
   (I *did* wonder whether it would count as legal
    If he pronounced me the wrong man's wife.)
But it wasn't the Southern Gothic bridal

     Sapped me, love; it was all I was consenting
  To: the life ahead we hope will use us fully,
    Wizening our bodies well as two liveoaks
Whose branches interlace fantastically
     Before they fail. Half-felled
   Myself, I stood below the courthouse chapel's
    Fairy-lit take on the Bower of Bliss,

Facing past the plastic fern to the abyss.
                    Nothing bridges it. But you
          Stood on its edge with me, grinning broader
                    Through your beard each time our tipsy
String-tied gentleman bluffly
                    Rechristened you. And seventy-five dollars
          Later, on the streetcar toward our fancy

                    Lunch for two: "It isn't every groom who'd eagerly
Give up his name. That makes you ... Mrs. *Who?*"
                    By then, you'd driven my existential vapors
          Off enough so I *could* laugh. And
          In spite of the humidity, the trolley
Chuckling fast along its tracks stirred up
                    A cheerful draft. On either side the trees

          Refreshed the street with sunshot shadows, so
                    We flashed giddily through alternate
Bright blinks and blacknesses. Somewhere
                    In the canopy, a woodpecker
          Uncorked his bubbling flute. Time felt
                    Suspended, balancing between symmetric
Poles where gravity is countered by

                    Velocity as, years before, our bodies
          Pressed together learned to take the hair-
                    Pin curves along a coastal cliff by gently
Leaning with the motorcycle's angle
                    Toward the road.
                                        Then you turned to me
          And, with a question, broke the spell. Remember
                    How I answered you? "I will. It's true. I am. I do."

Famously Beautiful City

For Nicole Cuddeback and Antonio Ambrosio

Thank Christ for outskirts where the river pulls you
East or west beyond brilliance into the simply making do,
Scrappy verges where the water eddies and people
Unremarkably rake their gardens or tinker under cars.

Please, please let's ignore the genius of the past today.

I need a walk with you along the margins where history's only
Years among friends and the only image of heaven
A glimpse of lemon trees beyond a rusty gate,
Someone burning trash in a yard and whistling.

Postscript

Of course nostalgia   Of course brooding

Give me the missing scattered through twelve states & four
    continents
Give me those scattered as ash

Give them their places at the table I have set
For them as much as for those gathered

How little it takes: a year   ten years
A shiver fast passing   & the eye clears

What once was love casts off disguises –
The cardinal's flame against forsythia simplified by snow –

What was love once spurns shallow guises & returns,
    startling,   as love

Notes

"Soft Power" quotes freely from Dickinson, Whitman, and Joseph Nye.

"The Monongahela Book of Hours." Three books I returned to through the years I lived in Pennsylvania informed my experience and the poems that came of it: Barbara Freese's *Coal: A Human History*, William Serrin's *Homestead: The Glory and Tragedy of An American Steel Town*, and Alexander Berkman's *Prison Letters of an Anarchist*.

A Note about the Author

Photo courtesy of Kristin Capp. © 2013

V. Penelope Pelizzon was born in 1967 in Massachusetts. Her first poetry collection, *Nostos* (2000), won the Hollis Summers Prize and the Poetry Society of America's Norma Farber First Book Award. She is also co-author of a critical study, *Tabloid, Inc.: Crimes, Newspapers, Narratives* (2010), and other essays on visual culture. Her poems have received the Amy Lowell Travelling Poetry Scholarship and a Discovery/*The Nation* Award, while her prose has twice been listed among the year's "notable essays" in the *Best American Essays* series. A diplomat's spouse, she navigates between postings abroad and her current position as Associate Professor of English at the University of Connecticut.